AMERICAN CORNERSTONES:

HISTORY'S INSIGHTS ON TODAY'S ISSUES

The Great American Experiment:
Evolution Of U.S. Taxation

by
JEFF BUSH

emerge
publishing

20 19 18   10 9 8 7 6 5 4 3 2

American Cornerstones: History's Insights on Today's Issues
THE GREAT AMERICAN EXPERIMENT:
EVOLUTION OF U.S. TAXATION

©2017 Jeff Bush

Published by:
Emerge Publishing, LLC
9521B Riverside Parkway, Suite 243
Tulsa, Oklahoma 74137
Phone: 888.407.4447
www.EmergePublishing.com

ISBN: 978-1-943127-67-2 Paperback
ISBN: 978-1-943127-68-9 Digital

BISAC Categories:
POL030000 POLITICAL SCIENCE / American Government / National
BUS064000 BUSINESS & ECONOMICS / Taxation / General

DISCLAIMER: This book is presented solely for educational purposes. The author and publisher are not offering it as tax, legal or financial advice. Neither is this work intended to sway the reader toward one model of tax reform over another, toward or away from any political party or persuasion. The intent is to make the reader think. If, by the last word of this book, the wheels of your mind are turning, then I've done my job as an author.

Printed in the United States of America.

INTRODUCTION

B uckle your seatbelt; you've just started reading a book about taxes. Perhaps no other word evokes more emotion from an American more quickly than the word "taxes." They've been called all sorts of things - levies, duties, tariffs, assessments, customs, tolls, tributes - but a tax by any other name is still a tax. Taxes have historically been viewed by at least a portion of Americans as a curb on their liberty and an intrusion of government into their lives. People have been tarred and feathered, stern letters have been written, punches have been thrown, a whole lot of tea found its way into a harbor, and wars have started over the issue of taxation.

A heated debate brewed regarding taxation from the earliest days of our nation - actually, before the United States of America even existed. Perhaps the debate is never more fevered than when the United States engages in the quadrennial process to elect its next president, but what many fail to realize is, it's not just federal taxation that dips into our wallets. Our local mayor can take a chunk out of our household budget as easily as the Spender in Chief of the United States. Taxes are imposed at many levels and take many forms in our nation.

So, what's a person to do? Thomas Jefferson was a great believer in the power of an educated and informed citizenry. In a letter to William Jarvis, Jefferson said, "I know no safe depository of the ultimate powers of the society but the people themselves; and if we think them not enlightened enough to exercise their control with a wholesome discretion, the remedy is not to take it from them, but to inform their discretion by education. This is the true corrective of abuses of constitutional power." We undertake this journey together to "inform our discretion" by educating ourselves on the history of taxation in the United States. This book is not political in nature; it will not advocate for one tax plan over another. It will only lay out the historical facts. I, like Jefferson, firmly believe that an educated electorate will make decisions that are in the best interest of our nation and her citizens.

As we begin, I'm going to assume that we agree that those who live under the protections of a government should contribute at least a little something for those protections. The free election of those who represent us is fundamentally American. Those elected representatives, in turn, have the responsibility to tax us "fairly."

With those givens in mind, the primary question is, how can a government most appropriately tax its citizenry?

- How much should a private citizen be expected to contribute?

- Should corporations bear part of the tax burden?

- How should taxes be assessed - on income, profits, inheritance, use, or some other way?

- Should tax rates be flat - one rate for all citizens? Or should rates be progressive, so those with a greater ability to pay are expected to bear a greater burden?

A look at these questions gives us an idea why development of a fair and proper taxation philosophy is such a conundrum. Perhaps an analysis of the successes and failures from our past can point us in the right direction as we seek to develop a more just system for raising necessary monies to fund programs for the common good. Obviously, there is no way to condense an 80,000-page tax code and 240 years of tax policy history into 100 pages. My intent is simply to move your understanding of tax philosophies and approaches forward. Hopefully, this work will help you be more discerning as we engage in tax reform dialogue.[1]

Very few people enjoyed their formal history education, therefore, they remember very little that they were taught.

★　　★　　★　　★　　★　　★　　★

"No government can exist
without taxation.

This money must necessarily be
levied on the people;

and the grand art consists of
levying so as not to oppress."

—Frederick the Great (1712-1786)
King of Prussia

★　　★　　★　　★　　★　　★　　★

★ ★ ★ ★ ★ ★ ★

"A traitor is everyone who does not agree with me."

—KING GEORGE III OF GREAT BRITAIN

(1738-1820)

★ ★ ★ ★ ★ ★ ★

ENGLAND TIGHTENS THE REINS

For more than a century, American colonists had enjoyed self-government and trade under the British Crown policy of salutary neglect, in which strict laws originally designed to keep the colonies in line were largely unenforced. Agricultural exports from the colonies to the Crown were booming, and colonists used their subsequent profits to import luxuries from England. But following the French and Indian War, a cash-strapped Great Britain now looked to their colonies to bear their fair share of the costs of the empire. The Crown owed money - lots of money - to British and Dutch bankers from whom they had borrowed heavily to fund the war, and the colonists were going to be called upon to help pay off the notes.

When Parliament passed the Revenue Act of 1762, it was a first step toward turning back the policy of salutary neglect. A significant provision of the act put British customs officials inside the colonies to actively collect duties on molasses and other sugar products that were heretofore routinely smuggled in duty-free from the French Sugar Islands in the subversion of the Molasses Act of 1733. Before enacting the Revenue Act, the customs service routinely collected only £2,000 of duties annually. After the passage of the Act, they raised upwards of £30,000 annually. But that wasn't enough to cut British losses and pay for the stationing of troops in the colonies. They would need more money, so in 1765, Prime Minister George Greenville and Parliament passed the Stamp Act.

The colonists did not like the Revenue Act of 1762 and the Sugar Act of 1764, but they tolerated them because they agreed it was the right of Parliament to regulate trade within the colonies. The Stamp Act, however, was an entirely different kind of revenue generating device. Under the Act, colonists were required to purchase stamps from the Crown that they then had to affix to products such as legal documents, playing cards, title deeds, and even newspapers. Colonists were required to pay for these stamps using British Sterling, not colonial paper money and British courts would enforce the Act, not provincial common law juries.

Colonists were vehemently opposed to the Stamp Act for a collection of reasons. First, this was a direct tax to generate revenue, not a usage tax (tariff). The levying of tariffs had the primary goal of controlling trade. If a citizen did not wish to pay the tariff, they did not purchase the taxable item. But as Ben Franklin noted in his address to Parliament in 1766, under the Stamp Act, if a person wanted to get married, buy or sell a property, pay debts or recover payment of debts, even if they died, they would have to pay the tax. You could not, by the process of your decisions, escape the tax.

Perhaps the strongest argument against the Stamp Act sprang from the fact that the legislative body enacting the measure had no colonist representation. Prime Minister Greenville claimed that the colonists had virtual representation in Parliament, but the colonists were not buying that argument. Up to that time, colonial legislatures made up of members elected by colonists held sole authority to put in place revenue taxes. Now with the Stamp Act, there was a political body an ocean away making decisions that affected every colonist's pocketbook. Arthur Lee of Virginia, when pointing out that none of the members of Parliament knew or were colonists themselves, went on to say, "Is he (the member of Parliament) bound in duty and interest to preserve our liberty and property? No. Is he acquainted with our circumstances, situations, wants, etc.? No. What then are we to expect from him? Nothing but taxes without end."

Patrick Henry, then a member of the Virginia House of Burgesses, proposed seven resolutions in opposition to the Stamp Act. He asserted that colonists were endowed with the same rights enjoyed by Englishmen in the home country. Among these was the right of colonists to be represented - not virtually, but actually represented - in any political body that might hold the power to enact taxation: "Resolved, that the taxation of the people by themselves, or by persons chosen by themselves to represent them, who can only know what taxes the people are able to bear, or the easiest method of raising them, and must themselves be affected by every tax laid on the people, is the only security against a burdensome taxation, and the distinguishing characteristic of British freedom, without which the ancient constitution cannot exist."

The Stamp Act brought the colonists together in a mutual commitment to resist the new tax. They brought their grievances to the Crown under the Stamp Act Resolves in which they decried the taxation without representation and respectfully requested the Act be repealed. The Colonists accompanied their words with actions. The Sons of Liberty, a secret organization formed to protest British taxation of the colonies, harassed stamp agents and tax collectors, burned tax collectors in effigy and ransacked homes of British officials. Colonists refused to purchase goods from Britain, putting in place a non-importation agreement. The agreement had its desired effect as it was widely adhered to across the colonies. Imports slowed dramatically. In 1766, the Stamp Act was repealed, but a Declaratory Act passed by Parliament reasserted the Crown's right to "bind the colonies and people of America... in all cases whatsoever." Parliament wanted to make it clear that the colonists might have won this battle and forced repeal of the Stamp Act, but the Crown had no intention of forgoing their right to tax their colonies in whatever ways they deemed appropriate.

A new administration came to power in Great Britain, led by Charles Townshend, Chancellor of the Exchequer. Townshend had not given up on the colonies as a source of revenue to ease the tax burden of those in the home country. In 1767, the Townshend Acts were passed to impose duties on glass, paint, lead, paper and tea. Though the duties were masked as "external" taxes (tariffs), which traditionally had been used to regulate commerce, colonists saw them for what they truly were - they were taxes designed to raise revenue just like the Stamp Act had been. The Sons of Liberty again sprang into action, calling for another non-importation agreement. By 1769, the non-importation agreement had once again worked its magic. Colonial exports exceeded imports, and the merchants back in England were crying for relief in the form of restored trade. The Townshend Acts were repealed in 1770, but a small duty on tea continued. The duty was quite small; it amounted to little more than a symbolic statement, Parliament's way of reminding the colonies that they could assert their right to tax them at any time they chose.

In 1773, Parliament, to shore up the failing East India Company, passed the Tea Act. Among other provisions, it allowed direct sales to the colonies, bypassing colonial merchants entirely. Because of the monopoly the East India Company now enjoyed in the tea market, their prices were always the lowest, even with the small duty the Crown imposed. Colonists saw this as an underhanded way for Parliament to exact taxes from the colonies. On December 16, 1773, colonists disguised as Native Americans boarded a British cargo ship and dumped 342 chests of East India Tea worth nearly $1 million in today's dollars, into Boston Harbor. The whole affair was very orderly, as the members of the tea party warned the ships' crews and customs officers to keep out of the way. The poorly disguised colonists were not a lawless mob, but rather a focused and deliberate group of patriots. The only loss suffered was the destruction of the tea. In fact, when it was discovered that the colonists had damaged one of the ship captain's personal padlocks, a replacement was brought from land and given to the captain as reimbursement for his loss. No persons were harmed in the action, and after its conclusion, the town of Boston slept soundly.

Let us be clear on the issues at stake. It is not that the duties imposed on the imported tea were excessive. They were not at all. It is not that the colonists didn't have the resources to pay the duties and were, therefore, forced to do without tea. No, this was a time of great affluence in the colonies. Ben Franklin said, "The ministry believe that threepence on a pound of tea, of which one does not perhaps drink ten pounds a year, is sufficient to overcome all the patriotism of an American." Money was not the motivation for the Boston Tea Party. It was something much more significant; the principle mattered more to the insurrectionists. John Adams said, "The question is whether the destruction of the tea was necessary? I apprehend it was absolutely and indispensably so…To let it be landed would be giving up the principle of taxation by Parliamentary authority, against which the continent has struggled for ten years."

Needless to say, the British government was not happy. In response, they passed the 1774 Coercive Acts (known in the colonies as the Intolerable Acts) to punish Massachusetts. The Acts consisted of four provisions. The port of Boston was to remain closed until damages from the tea party were repaid. Parliament placed restrictions on democratic gatherings in Massachusetts. British officials were now immune from prosecution in Massachusetts, and the Quartering Act required colonists to house and quarter British troops on demand, including housing them in the colonists' private homes. If Parliament thought that would crush the rebellion, they could not have been more wrong. In response, the First Continental Congress met. By 1776, the Declaration of Independence landed at the feet of the Crown. The newly declared United States of America denied that British Parliament had the right to exercise any authority over the colonies at all.

★ ★ ★ ★ ★ ★ ★

"It is essential that you should practically bear in mind

that towards the payment of debts there must be revenue;

that to have revenue there must be taxes;

that no taxes can be devised which are not more or less inconvenient and unpleasant."

— George Washington (1732-1799)

1st President of the United States

From his Farewell Address of 1796

★ ★ ★ ★ ★ ★ ★

★ ★ ★ ★ ★ ★ ★

*"The power of taxing people
and their property
is essential to the very
existence of government."*

— JAMES MADISON (1751-1836)

4TH PRESIDENT OF THE UNITED STATES

★ ★ ★ ★ ★ ★ ★

TAXATION IN A FLEDGLING NATION

On November 15, 1777, the Continental Congress passed the Articles of Confederation for the new United States of America, creating a loose confederation of highly independent states. In fact, states pretty much retained their sovereignty in all areas except diplomacy and defense. The Articles of Confederation did not give the central government the power to tax the states or their citizens; the states themselves held that exclusive right. After their experience with Parliament and the Crown, it is understandable that Americans would have been leery of entrusting the new central government with too much power to tax. Each state had a suggested amount they were asked to contribute to the federal coffers, but Congress had no authority to collect, by force, those amounts. As should have been expected, most states only sent a portion of their suggested contribution, if they sent anything at all.

Failures of the independent states to send in their suggested federal contributions hurt the war effort. Revolutionary soldiers fought through the winter barefoot in the snow because there was no money to outfit the troops properly. Many soldiers succumbed to frostbite. Supply lines were slim to non-existent, so men on the front lines were starving. The fledgling nation was having trouble paying its creditors. In 1780, Alexander Hamilton warned, "Without revenues, a government can have no power. That power which holds the purse strings absolutely must rule." There had to be a way to raise revenues while at the same time, preserve the idea that no American citizen would be subjected to taxation without representation in the political body imposing the taxes.

In 1787, a draft of the new Constitution granted the national legislature the exclusive power to impose tariffs and gave them the ability to assess taxes on the citizenry (while preserving a state's right to tax their citizens).

Article 1, Section 8 of the Constitution reads, "The Congress shall have Power To lay and collect Taxes, Duties, Imposts and Excises, to pay the Debts and provide for the common Defense and general Welfare of the United States; but all Duties, Imposts, and Excises shall be uniform throughout the United States."

Article 1, Section 7 of the Constitution specified initiation of all revenue bills begin in the House of Representatives - the people's house. By allocating House seats based on population, it guarantees citizens equal representation in the taxing body of our government.

Article 1, Section 9 of the Constitution says, "No Capitation or other direct Tax shall be laid, unless in Proportion to the Census or enumeration herein before directed to be taken." The 16th Amendment to the Constitution deals with the proportionality issue, and we will discuss that later in the book, but I think we need to clarify at this point what constitutes a "direct tax" and how it is different from an "indirect tax." A direct tax is defined as a tax levied on a person's income and wealth. The tax burden cannot be shifted to anyone else - the one who owes it has to pay it. Direct taxes include such things as income tax, property tax, or corporate taxes. By and large, one cannot avoid direct taxes. If I make money from any source, I'm subject to direct taxes.

An indirect tax, on the other hand, is a tax levied on a person who consumes goods. The burden of indirect taxes can be shifted to someone else. For instance, if I am a wine importer and I am assessed an indirect tax (a tariff) for importing that wine, I can pass that tax burden along to the people who buy my wine by just charging a bit more for each bottle. In addition to tariffs, examples of indirect taxes include sales taxes, value added taxes and customs duties for international travelers. I can avoid indirect taxes. If I don't want to pay the tax, I just pass the burden along to my customers.

If my clients don't want to pay the higher price, they can purchase a domestic bottle of wine and avoid the higher priced, imported, wine. Remember this distinction when you hear discussions about tariffs and border adjustment taxes.

If you recall, Americans have never truly disputed a government's right to levy indirect taxes as a means of both regulating trade and raising revenue. However, Americans have been hesitant to allow any centralized government to tax them directly. Patrick Henry was one of the most vocal opponents of allowing for direct federal taxation under the new Constitution. He held to the idea that state governments were most familiar with their residents and therefore, best suited to know what forms and amounts of taxation those people would be able to bear. He said, "The oppression arising from taxation, is not to the amount but, from the mode - a thorough acquaintance with the condition of the people, is necessary to a just distribution of taxes." Henry believed that the interests of the people from his home state of Virginia would be overshadowed as representatives from the many colonies all sought to protect the interests of their constituents. Only Virginians would do what was best for Virginia. Therefore, only Virginians should be allowed to levy direct taxes on their fellow Virginians.

The first U.S. Secretary of the Treasury, Alexander Hamilton, had a much different opinion. He believed if the new nation was to survive, the federal government must not only be allowed to enact tariffs and other forms of indirect tax, but the federal government also should be given the privilege of raising revenue by whatever means the representatives deemed fair and acceptable. He said, "A nation cannot long exist without revenues. Destitute of this essential support, it must resign its independence, and sink into the degraded condition of a province. This is an extremity to which no government will of choice accede." Though he believed indirect taxes would provide the lion's share of revenues, direct taxes were, in his mind, just another option for filling government coffers in times of need.

Hamilton's argument was persuasive. The new Constitution, including provisions for Congress to directly tax the populace, was officially established as the governing document of the United States on June 21, 1788. For decades after, however, tariffs would still account for 90 percent of federal government revenue.

In 1791, to raise revenue to reduce the national debt following the Revolutionary War, the federal government imposed its first tax on a domestic product when it began to tax distilled spirits. At the time, whiskey was by far the most consumed of the distilled spirits, so this tax is often referred to as the Whiskey Tax. Secretary of the Treasury Hamilton believed this "luxury" or "sin" tax would be the least offensive means for the government to raise revenue. He was wrong. Immediately, the tax met resistance on the western frontier where farmers often distilled their excess grain into whiskey, and some even used the spirit as a medium of exchange. Frontier residents petitioned for repeal of the tax, and when their non-violent measures failed, more radical steps followed. Tax evaders whipped, tarred and feathered the tax collectors. Even those not actively involved in the collection of the tax were targeted. If any individual so much as cooperated with the tax, they were subjected to denigration.

It did not matter that the tax went largely uncollected. The fact that the law was still on the books encouraged opponents to the measure to continue their protests, many of which had grown increasingly violent. At the Battle of Bower Hill, tax protestors surrounded the home of General John Neville, federal tax inspector for western Pennsylvania. Though it is unclear exactly how many may have fallen in the standoff, historical accounts confirm there were multiple casualties. On August 1, 1794, 7,000 people gathered at Braddock's Field to protest the Whiskey Tax (though the protests had expanded to encompass all manner of economic grievances). There was some talk of marching on Pittsburgh to loot the homes of the wealthy and set fire to the town. There was some discussion of secession by declaring independence from the United States. In the spirit of the French Revolution, some called for the guillotine. Though none of these extreme measures ultimately were taken, President George Washington had seen enough of the tax protests. It was time to act.

President Washington sent envoys to meet with the dissenters to hear their grievances, even as he set about raising a militia to march west to put down the rebellion. On August 4, 1794, Washington advised the protestors that they had until September 1 to disperse. The militia was on their way west. When the troops arrived, there were minor flare ups of rebellion, but there were no widespread instances of violence. By October 1794, the rebellion had collapsed entirely.

The Whiskey Tax was eventually repealed by Thomas Jefferson when he took office. It had become nothing more than a tax façade, in that very little revenues were collected. However, the events surrounding the tax were significant. If there had been a question before about the legitimacy of the new government and her willingness and ability to enforce tax law, Washington's response to the protestors settled any doubt that the new federal government would act when necessary.

The nation continued to move along with revenues from tariffs footing the bill for operation of the federal government. During the War of 1812, a minor skirmish the United States engaged in against Great Britain, Secretary of the Treasury Alexander Dallas proposed a direct tax on income to raise money for the war effort. There was little support for his proposal, and the war ended before the tax went into effect.

★ ★ ★ ★ ★ ★ ★

"What at first was plunder assumed the softer name of revenue."

— THOMAS PAINE (1737-1809)

FOUNDING FATHER

★ ★ ★ ★ ★ ★ ★

★ ★ ★ ★ ★ ★ ★

"No nation was ever ruined by trade, even seemingly the most disadvantageous."

— Benjamin Franklin (1706-1790)

Founding Father

★ ★ ★ ★ ★ ★ ★

* * * * * * *

"An unlimited power to tax involves, necessarily, the power to destroy."

— DANIEL WEBSTER (1782-1852)

UNITED STATES SENATOR

* * * * * * *

RUN UP TO THE WAR BETWEEN THE STATES

Embargoes imposed on foreign products during the War of 1812 (1812-1815) caused Americans to rely more heavily on domestically produced products. At the end of the war, the government sought to encourage the continued growth of these domestic industries through the enactment of protectionist tariffs (high taxes on imports and exports). The Tariff Act of 1816 imposed a series of 20 to 25 percent tariffs on a variety of products.

As with so many things financial, you have to strike a careful balance. The government needs to ensure that when enacting tariffs to protect domestic industries (and fill government coffers), they do not harm the consumers who have to purchase products and services.

When a country enacts a protectionist tariff, it helps domestic manufacturers. By adding a tax on top of the cost of imported goods, suddenly domestic products are a bargain. Protectionist tariffs protect domestic producers against an influx to the market of cheap foreign products.

As you would imagine, foreign producers are hurt by protectionist tariffs. Their revenue decreases as foreign demand for their products decreases.

But what of the consumer? Protectionist tariffs decrease consumer surplus. The definition of consumer surplus is the difference between what consumers are willing and able to pay for a good or service and what they have to pay (the market price of the good or service). For example, if an individual is prepared to pay $250 for a new chair, but it retails for $200, it creates a $50 consumer surplus. Consumer surplus is not so much an issue of actual dollars and cents that remain in the pocket, as it is a matter of good feeling. If a consumer feels they are getting a good deal, they have a positive feeling about the market. At the risk of being too simplistic, it's fair to say that feeling good (optimism) makes for better economies.

Protectionist tariffs increase consumer prices, which means consumer surplus decreases. To some degree, consumers are willing to pay higher prices if they perceive more utility from a product or service - if they believe, even at the higher price, it is still a good value. But go too far with protectionist tariffs, and consumer feelings turn dark; at that point, consumers may just rebel.

Congress considered additional tariffs in 1820 and 1824 - Congress enacted some, others not - but a wave of protectionist sentiment was gaining momentum. In 1828, a proposed schedule would have increased tariffs on many items such as hemp, fur, wool, flax, liquor and imported textiles to nearly 50percent. The Tariff of 1828 - called the Tariff of Abominations in the South - was eventually passed.

The South was beside itself. The Southern economy was based primarily on cotton and slaves, so a majority of products citizens in the South depended on were imported. Southerners imported most of their clothing, most of their farm implements, even a good deal of their food. With this increase in tariffs, Southerners would be paying more for these goods. But the problems for the South didn't stop there. Thanks to the sharp increase in tariffs on exports, trade partners in Europe began looking elsewhere to find supplies of cotton, indigo, and rice (the primary exports from the South). It seemed to Southerners that while the Northern industrialists got fatter with each new tariff, their way of life and economy in the South deteriorated.

While some in the South were calling for secession from the Union over the Tariff of Abominations, John Calhoun of South Carolina - formerly a senator, now the vice president of the United States - argued the doctrine of nullification applied. The doctrine of nullification, first set forth by Thomas Jefferson and James Madison in the Kentucky and Virginia Resolutions of 1799, is the idea that states can and must declare null and void and refuse to enforce any law they deem unconstitutional. Since Southerners believed that the tariffs effectively worked to seize wealth from the South and redistribute it to Northern manufacturing interests, Calhoun argued that the tariffs were unconstitutional because they were discriminatory in failing to provide equal benefits to all Americans. Since (by Calhoun's reasoning) the law was unconstitutional, states had the right to convene nullification conventions for the purpose of nullifying the law within their state's borders. In "South Carolina Exposition and Protest," Calhoun went on to say that if three-fourths of the rest of the states disagreed with a state's invocation of the doctrine of nullification and instead, affirmed the right of the federal government to enforce the law the state believed to be unconstitutional, the disagreeing state had the right to seceded from the Union. A standoff had commenced.

In 1832, Congress lowered tariff rates somewhat but kept high rates on manufactured cloth. Many in the South saw this as yet another slap in the face. In November, South Carolina's Nullification Convention declared the tariffs of 1828 and 1832 unconstitutional. As far as South Carolina was concerned, these tariff laws did not exist.

President Andrew Jackson responded to this action by South Carolina in two ways. First, he called for reductions in tariffs across the board starting in 1833.

These were called the Compromise Tariffs. Second, he worked for passage of the Force Bill, which authorized the president to use both the army and the navy, if necessary, to enforce the law (in this case, to collect tariffs throughout all of the Union - even South Carolina). Because of the reduction in tariffs, South Carolina was able to back down from their hardline stance while saving face. For the time being, the Union was preserved.

In the years that followed, government revenues ebbed and flowed as the economy went through cycles. By and large, tariff rates remained low. But then came the Civil War, which threw tariff rates back up into the stratosphere.

"War involves in its progress such a train of unforeseen circumstances

that no human wisdom can calculate the end;

it has but one thing certain, and that is to increase taxes."

— THOMAS PAINE (1737-1809)

FOUNDING FATHER

"What the government gives it must first take away."

— John S. Coleman (1926-1995)

American sociologist, theorist, and

researcher

WAR IS AN EXPENSIVE UNDERTAKING

From the outset of the Civil War, the Confederate states were playing catch up. In 1861, the year the first shots were fired in the Civil War, the South possessed only 18 percent of the nation's industrial capacity, even though 42 percent of the country's population lived there.[1] The South had to import uniforms and boots for their soldiers, armaments, and even a great deal of their food. The incredibly high tariff rates made prices for these goods astronomical. Since the focus of this book is taxation, we won't launch into a lengthy debate over the causes of the Civil War. I do, however, think it is safe to say that the South had their pocketbooks in mind when they were considering engaging in the fight.

With the budgets of their citizens already tight, the Confederate Congress was loathed to enact a system of

---

1   Steven R. Weisman, *The Great Tax Wars: Lincoln-Teddy Roosevelt-Wilson, How the Income Tax Transformed America* (New York: Simon & Schuster, 2002), 52.

increased taxation to generate revenue. They preferred instead to print additional money and use that to pay their bills. During the first year of the war, the Confederate States derived only two percent of their revenue from taxes. Though that percentage would increase slightly during the next two years, the printing of paper money made up the lion's share of revenue. The problem with this, however, was that the more money they printed, the higher inflation rose. Southern currency became devalued because there was more and more of it floating around. Even with a growing scarcity of goods, the value of Southern currency kept decreasing. A pair of shoes that cost one Confederate dollar in 1861, cost 25 Confederate dollars in 1863.

Finally, in April 1863, the Confederate government imposed a progressive income tax with rates that varied based on how the individuals earned income. Income from salaries was taxed at one rate, while income derived from other sources was taxed at another rate. The revenue bill also included provisions for excise taxes (indirect taxes on the purchase of specific items), license taxes and a profits tax on wholesalers. To both feed the troops and raise some much-needed revenue, the legislation also included a 10 percent tax-in-kind on agricultural products. A tax-in-kind meant that farmers were required to give 10 percent of their crops to the government. Farmers saw this as very unfair. Whereas office workers could pay their tax bill using worthless Confederate currency, farmers had to give over valuable commodities (crops, livestock, etc.). These fiscal measures were not well received. Because certain large plantations and slaves continued to be exempt from taxation, the general populace was of the opinion that the war was being fought on the backs of poor men to preserve the rich plantation owner's way of life.

The tax bill of 1863 didn't come close to raising enough revenue for the money strapped Confederacy. In February of 1864, Confederate lawmakers imposed a five percent tax on all property, including the value of all land and slaves. They also raised the minimum income tax rate to 25 percent. In June 1864, they raised tax rates again, including increasing the sales tax rate by an additional 30 percent. Just before the end of the war, the Confederate legislature again tried to raise tax rates, but it was too late. The Confederacy was broke, and before the imposition of new taxes, General Lee surrendered.

****

On the eve of the Civil War, 92 percent of all U.S. government revenue came by way of tariffs. The American people were not accustomed to giving anything to their government outside of indirect taxes like tariffs. As the war began and the Union had to raise funds to support their fighting forces, tariffs gradually climbed. Americans in the Union were paying more for just about everything they purchased than they had ever paid before. Meanwhile, owners of manufacturing facilities who produced goods needed to fight the war were making money hand over fist.

To show the American people that all citizens were bearing some of the burdens of the war to preserve the Union, Congress enacted the first ever income tax, as well as levied taxes on corporations. The income tax was seen as superior to additional taxes on commodities, in that the burden would fall on each man according to his ability to pay. It was considered superior to a tax on real property, in that those wealthy Americans who had opted to put their money into stocks and bonds rather than real property would still be asked to pay their fair share.

On July 1, 1862, President Abraham Lincoln signed a sweeping revenue bill. Included in that bill was the first income tax measure. It enacted a tax of three percent on incomes over $600 and five percent on incomes over $10,000. (Keep in mind, the average household income at this time was $450 or less, so few people were subject to the tax.) The tax was to apply to "annual gains, profits or incomes of any person residing in the United States, whether derived from any kind of property, rents, interest, dividends, salaries or from any profession, trade, employment of vocation carried on in the United States or elsewhere, or from any source whatever." The law established the Internal Revenue Board that would collect the tax. It also established provisions for tax collection by employers.

Also in 1862, the Morrill Tariff Act was passed, which raised tariffs significantly. Representative Justin Smith Morrill of Vermont, the sponsor of the tariff bill, argued that these protective tariffs would serve as a balm to those wealthy industrialists in the North who were, perhaps, most hard hit by the new income tax. He said, "If we bleed manufacturers, we must see to it that the proper tonic is administered at the same time. Otherwise, we shall destroy the goose that lays the golden egg."

In the first year the income tax was in place, the Revenue Board collected $39.1 million (over $930 million in today's dollars). George S. Boutwell was tapped by Lincoln to be the first Commissioner of Internal Revenue, and he and his staff were tasked with setting policy and regulations for the organization. If there was a question about whether or not something was taxable, Boutwell and his collaborators would discuss the matter at the end of the day and arrive at a consensus. What they decided became policy. The Bureau was made up of assessors and collectors. Assessors gave out instructions and determined how much each taxpayer owed. Collectors were in the field receiving the revenue. Officials working in both of these positions received bonuses based on the amounts they collected. (Does anyone else see a problem with that arrangement?)

Proceeds from the 1862 tax fell short of what the Union needed to continue to fight the war, so in 1864, Congress revised the income tax. The revised income tax established new brackets and rates:

Income of $0-$599	0%
Income of $600-$5000	5%
Income of $5001-$10,000	7.5%
Income >$10,000	10%

Morrill once again contended that tariffs should be raised along with these increases in income tax rates. He managed to convince Congress to raise tariffs to 47 percent. Imagine being an American at that time. You are now subject to a never-before-seen direct tax (income tax) while you are also paying tariffs of forty-seven percent on the products you use every day!

In February 1865 with the war continuing, Congress again tweaked the income tax rates. The lower bracket remained the same - 5 percent on incomes from $600 to $5,000 - but now any income over $5,000 would be taxed at the highest rate of ten percent. Not many months later, in April 1865, General Lee surrendered at Appomattox Court House and the war was over. Though there was still the matter of war debt that had to be retired, the wealthy were growing ever more insistent that the wartime taxes should be eliminated. The repeal of the income tax and inheritance tax came within seven years of the end of the war.

****

What tax lessons can we learn from the way the North and the South each financed their war efforts? Obviously, the South was at an economic disadvantage from the outset, simply because of the agrarian makeup of their economy. They could not produce the products they needed domestically, so they had to look to outside sources to supply their troops and their citizens, and the tariffs they had to pay had a crippling effect on their finances. Northerners did not escape high tariffs, but they were not burdened nearly to the same extent as those in the South. The North had a good number of domestic manufacturers who could produce products and save the citizens from paying high tariffs on imported goods. Perhaps what we take away from our study of the difference in experience between the North and the South in this one aspect is the importance of establishing vibrant and diverse domestic industries to reduce dependence on imports.

There can be no question that the South operated, at least at first, with a firm commitment to states' rights, such as had been put forth under the Articles of Confederation, while the Union operated with a much stronger centralized federal government. But did this affect the outcome of the war? Just as it had done to Washington's troops during the Revolutionary War, failure to have a strong federal government that could impose and collect taxes to fund the war effort hurt the Confederate military. By the time the Confederate legislature realized the peril their fiscal policies had created, it was too late. Runaway inflation plagued the South, and there was simply not enough wealth in the South to overcome the problem. Not to say, with proper funding, the Southern war effort outcome would have been any different, but the lack of finances brought on by a failure of the government to establish and enforce a reasonable tax policy certainly didn't help.

✮　✮　✮　✮　✮　✮　✮

"A democratic government is the only one in which those who vote for a tax

can escape the obligation to pay it."

— ALEXIS DE TOCQUEVILLE (1805–1859)

FRENCH HISTORIAN

✮　✮　✮　✮　✮　✮　✮

☆ ☆ ☆ ☆ ☆ ☆ ☆

"You cannot bring about
prosperity by discouraging
thrift.

You cannot help small men by
tearing down big men.

You cannot strengthen the weak
by weakening the strong.

You cannot lift the wage-earner
by pulling down the wage-payer.

You cannot help the poor man
by destroying the rich.

You cannot keep out of trouble
by spending more than your
income.

*You cannot further the
brotherhood of man by inciting
class hatred.*

*You cannot establish security on
borrowed money.*

*You cannot build character and
courage by taking away men's
initiative and independence.*

*You cannot help men
permanently by doing for them
what they could and should do
for themselves."*

— Rev. William Boetcker (1873-1962)

Presbyterian Minister

THE COST OF REBUILDING

Conservative estimates state that the Civil War cost the North anywhere from $5 billion to $6 billion to wage. At the end of the war, the North had nearly $3 billion in war debt, including expenses for soldier pensions and repayment of war bonds sold during the conflict.

For those who had helped finance the Union war effort, it was time to reap the income from the investments they made in war bonds. But follow this line of thought, more often than not, only the wealthiest Americans had enough money during the Civil War to purchase war bonds. The income tax program passed during the Civil War was progressive in nature (the higher your income, the more tax you paid), with those making less than $600 entirely exempt from taxation. The low household income levels at that time meant only about 250,000 people out of a total population of 39.5 million (.64% of the population) were paying taxes. So, only the wealthiest were paying taxes to enable the government to make good on the war bonds they sold to the wealthiest during the Civil War. The rich were paying themselves back for their investment!

But, what else was the government to do? This money was owed to the bond holders. If the government eliminated the income tax, the only other real source of revenue would be tariffs. That would mean the Average Joe's household budget would take the hit to foot the bill so the wealthy could get wealthier. Was it fair to make the average person now pay for a war that was fought so the wealthy could continue to enjoy their standard of living?

Congress made adjustments to the tax brackets so fewer and fewer people were affected by the income tax, leaving only the income of the most wealthy 100,000 Americans subject to taxation. In the end, the income tax was repealed, partly because the wealthy argued it was not fair to make them bear so much of the burden and in part because it was determined that it was just not worth it to administer such a complex system to collect revenue from so few. Also, evidence of waste and abuse by the government was widely publicized during this time, bringing widespread support to the argument that the tax program needed to go. By 1872, the income tax was abolished.

Once the income tax was gone, government revenue primarily came from tariffs. The burden of raising the revenue to retire government debt, now depended on the consumption habits of the working man. How could a congressman (because they were all men until 1917) spin a tariff as a positive thing for his constituents? We know how congresspeople love to deliver news of great new projects or sources of revenue to their home districts. The congressmen of those days had a game of working to have a new protective tariff passed. Then, they would tell their constituents how they worked to save the home region's industry through these protective tariffs.

In the years following the repeal of the first income tax, America thrived in the tariff system - so much so that the federal government enjoyed years of surplus. Though there were occasional tariff reductions, for the most part, tariff rates steadily climbed. In 1890, the McKinley Tariff pushed rates to an all-time high.

Congress had apparently gone too far. The McKinley Tariff was too much for the American public to stomach. In the next congressional elections, the Republican party that had pushed through the McKinley Tariff suffered heavy losses. In the 1892 presidential election, Grover Cleveland, a champion of tariff reform, was sent to the White House.

In 1894, the Wilson-Gorman Tariff passed legislative scrutiny. For those hoping for tariff reduction, the bill was a colossal disappointment, as only slightly lower duties ensued. The tariff system continued to place the burden of financing the government squarely on the shoulders of the working poor. While wealthy Americans contributed 8 to 10 percent of their earnings to finance the government, the poor were spending 75 to 80 percent of their income on tariffed goods.[2] However, the new tariff act did include one interesting provision – a modest income tax of 2% on incomes over $4,000. The economic depression of 1893 had hit middle and lower income households hard, causing the divide between rich and poor to grow tremendously. Perhaps this growing income gap made the country ready for another run at the income tax. Benton McMillan, Democrat from Tennessee, had this to say about the new federal income tax provision in the Wilson-Gorman Bill: "I ask of any reasonable person whether it is unjust to expect that a small percent of this enormous revenue shall be placed upon the accumulated wealth of the country instead of placing all upon the consumption of the people…My friends, are we going to put all of this burden on the things men eat and wear and leave out those vast accumulations of wealth?"

But, this is politics, so you know there was opposition to the measure. Both Democrats and Republicans from the Northeast were widely opposed to the income tax. High exemption rates meant that nearly 90 percent of people paid no taxes. Critics of the measure asserted that because so few would be called upon to pay, those few who did contribute would be able to exert undue influence on the government. They also

2   Steven R. Weisman, *The Great Tax Wars: Lincoln-Teddy Roosevelt-Wilson: How the Income Tax Transformed America* (New York: Simon & Schuster, 2002), 123.

suggested the income tax would encourage fraud, as the wealthy would falsify their financials to avoid paying the tax. Opponents also charged the wealthy would flee the country and live elsewhere, rather than subject themselves to the income tax.

In the end, the Wilson-Gorman Bill was passed, allowing the income tax collection from both corporations and individuals for five years. But, no sooner had the bill passed, a court challenge ensued. In the landmark Supreme Court case *Pollock v. Farmers' Loan and Trust Co.*, the Supreme Court ruled that the income tax provision of the Wilson-Gorman Bill was unconstitutional because it was a direct tax and therefore, subject to the apportionment clause of the Constitution.

Further comment on the apportionment clause might be useful here. Article 1, Section 2, Clause 3 of the U.S. Constitution is where you can find the apportionment clause: "Representatives and direct Taxes shall be apportioned among the several States which may be included within this Union, according to their respective Numbers…." Any direct taxation had to be properly apportioned among the various states of the Union. (Remember our definition from earlier - a direct tax is one that cannot be avoided by changing your buying habits and you can't avoid that tax burden by passing it along to anyone else. With that definition in mind, it is clear to see that the income tax was a direct tax.) Adherence to the apportionment clause would mean that if a state made up 10% of the nation's population, they could only be required to pay 10% of all income taxes collected. Since there was not a fixed sum to be raised by the income tax, it was impossible to apportion the tax burden between the states correctly. Since apportionment was impossible, the Supreme Court had no choice but to strike down the income tax as unconstitutional.

Another result of the economic depression of 1893 was to force the government into a budget deficit. With the income tax now off the table, new tariffs were passed to generate the necessary revenue. The Dingley Tariff drove rates to an all-time high. When the government needed new revenues with the onset of the Spanish-American War, a national inheritance tax came into being. This tax was progressive, taxing larger estates more heavily. Perhaps the most noteworthy thing about these new inheritance taxes is the fact that they survived in the courts, with the Supreme Court ruling that the tax was not subject to the apportionment clause and the progressive nature of the tax did not violate any Constitutional rules of uniformity.

Though the government had added the additional revenue stream of the inheritance tax, the system of heavy tariffs remained. The ever-increasing tariffs started to heap a double burden on everyday Americans. Not only were they paying higher costs for goods they used every day, but as foreign markets became increasingly upset with the high tariffs assessed against their goods by America, they began to retaliate by refusing to purchase exports from America. American farmers and manufacturers felt the pinch in this tug-of-war.

★ ★ ★ ★ ★ ★ ★

"Taxes are paid in the sweat of every man who labors."

— FRANKLIN D. ROOSEVELT (1882-1945)

32ND PRESIDENT OF THE UNITED STATES

★ ★ ★ ★ ★ ★ ★

★ ★ ★ ★ ★ ★ ★

"The hardest thing in the world to understand is the income tax."

— ALBERT EINSTEIN (1879-1955)

THEORETICAL PHYSICIST

★ ★ ★ ★ ★ ★ ★

✫ ✫ ✫ ✫ ✫ ✫ ✫

"Income from illegal activities,
such as money from dealing
illegal drugs,

must be included in your income
on Form 1040, line 21."

ACTUAL IRS TAX PUBLICATION

HTTPS://WWW.IRS.GOV/PUBLICATIONS/P17/
CH12.HTML

✫ ✫ ✫ ✫ ✫ ✫ ✫

THE ROAD TO THE 16TH
AMENDMENT

President Teddy Roosevelt, who first became president in September 1901 following the assassination of William McKinley, began boldly speaking about the duty of the wealthiest Americans to pay their share to fund the government "in a spirit of entire justice and moderation." At first, he suggested an even more progressive inheritance tax, but then Roosevelt turned to discussions of a general progressive income tax. However, Roosevelt put forward no specific proposals, and while acknowledging the Supreme Court's ruling striking down an income tax in 1895, he offered no solutions to work around that ruling. In his book *Tax Wars*, Steven Weisman says that Roosevelt felt "the income tax was clearly a cause for which he was prepared to take a stand, but not to stake his presidency."[3]

---

3   Steven R. Weisman, *The Great Tax Wars: Lincoln-Teddy Roosevelt-Wilson: How the Income Tax Transformed America* (New York: Simon & Schuster, 2002), 206.

Though Roosevelt opted not to run for a second term in the presidency, he did make sure to hand-pick his successor. William Howard Taft took office in 1909 with the debate over the enactment of an income tax still going strong. Multiple proposals for a new income tax were put forth from both sides of the aisle but ultimately, Taft did not want to deal with the court challenge that he knew would certainly ensue should any personal income tax measure be put into law. Therefore, he worked with members of Congress to pass a one percent tax on corporate income. This certainly wouldn't solve the revenue problems facing the government, but at least it was something. The bill was intentionally worded in such a way as to sidestep any potential constitutional issues.

During negotiations for the corporate income tax, one concession Taft made was an agreement to throw his support behind a constitutional amendment establishing a federal personal income tax. With the president backing the action - or at least not outright opposing it - Congress proposed the Sixteenth Amendment to the Constitution and a number of state legislatures quickly ratified it. Alabama was the first state to ratify, followed in short order by Georgia, Illinois, Kentucky, Maryland, Mississippi, Oklahoma and Texas. Many of these states already had state income tax provisions on the books.

But, not everyone was so quick to jump onboard the amendment train. Opponents of the Sixteenth

Amendment and the tax it would allow were passionate and vocal. Some opposed the tax because they did not feel it was right to confiscate income from a person simply because they had it to take; some saw it as opening the door wide to government overreach. Consider these words from Richard E. Byrd, speaker of the Virginia House of Delegates:

> *A hand from Washington will be stretched out and placed upon every man's business; the eye of the Federal inspector will be in every man's counting house... The law will of necessity have inquisitorial features; it will provide penalties, it will create complicated machinery. Under it, men will be drug into courts distant from their homes. Heavy fines imposed by distant and unfamiliar tribunals will constantly menace the taxpayer. An army of Federal inspectors, spies and detectives will descend upon the state... Who of us who have had knowledge of the doings of the Federal officials in the Internal Revenue service can be blind to what will follow?*

Though opposition was intense, the time of the income tax had apparently come. On February 3, 1913, the amendment was ratified by a thirty-sixth state legislature, pushing the measure over the three-fourths mark to officially make it law. Now that the law was on the books, it was up to the new president, who would be taking office in just a few weeks to enact it.

Shortly after taking office, President Woodrow Wilson called for revenue reform. The bill that passed both houses of Congress in short order lowered tariff rates considerably and enacted an income tax of one percent on income over $3,000 ($4,000 for married couples). Average household income at this time was $577, so the new income tax was only estimated to affect the wealthiest 3% in the nation (approximately 425,000 individuals). There was an additional progressive surtax on higher incomes. Representative Cordell Hull of Tennessee was a champion of this new tax bill. When answering those critics who said that the new income tax would encourage an increase in federal spending, Hull countered that an income tax would encourage restraint in government spending because legislators would respect the fact that they were spending money taken directly from hard working Americans. I'll just leave that thought there and allow you to ruminate on whether or not Hull was correct in his assumption.

Under previous incarnations of the income tax, returns were made public. Under this new law, returns would be kept private. In 1914, the Bureau of Internal Revenue published the forms that would need to be completed to file under the new income tax law. Form 1040 was four pages long.

"Congress can raise taxes because it can persuade a sizable fraction of the populace that somebody else will pay."

— MILTON FRIEDMAN (1912-2006)

AMERICAN ECONOMIST AND NOBEL PRIZE

WINNER

★　　★　　★　　★　　★　　★　　★

"The difference between death and taxes is

death doesn't get worse every time Congress meets."

— WILL ROGERS (1879-1935)

AMERICAN ACTOR, HUMORIST, AND SOCIAL

COMMENTATOR

★　　★　　★　　★　　★　　★　　★

"No government ever voluntarily reduces itself in size.

Government programs, once launched, never disappear.

Actually, a government bureau is the nearest thing to eternal life

we'll ever see on this earth!"

— RONALD REAGAN (1911-2004)

40TH PRESIDENT OF THE UNITED STATES

SETTLING IN WITH
THE NEW TAX LAW

With the outbreak of World War I and the United States' imminent entry into the fight, additional revenue was needed to fund the war effort. When consumption taxes failed to raise enough additional funding, calls to increase income tax rates came. The Revenue Act of 1916 doubled the tax rate on those earning over $3,000 ($4,000 for married couples), from one to two percent. Surtax rates on larger incomes also nearly doubled.

Still, war finance remained at the forefront of everyone's mind. Claude Kitchin, the representative from North Carolina, put forward the idea of a corporate excess profits tax. This excess profits tax would be assessed on any corporate profits above an established reasonable rate of return. Of course, Congress would determine what rate of return was "reasonable." Kitchin's proposal was to tax net corporate income at 8 percent, after an exemption of $5,000. The bill passed and was signed into law in March of 1917. Later in

1917, the War Revenue Act increased corporate and personal income tax rates.

The expansion of the tax base through the enactment of various forms of taxation and the subsequent increase in revenue flowing into the federal treasury precipitated a drastic increase in the number of bureaucrats working at the Bureau of Internal Revenue. In 1917, the Bureau employed 5,053 people. By 1918, the number employed had grown to 9,600. By 1922, the agency employed nearly 21,000 people. During this time, the number of tax returns filed increased almost 1,000 percent. Income taxes as a percentage of federal revenue climbed from 16 percent in 1916 to 58 percent in 1920.

At the end of World War I, the Revenue Act of 1918 passed, which set the top tax rate at 77 percent. Think about that - the government was confiscating more than three-fourths of a person's income if that person happened to earn over a certain amount.

The verbiage in discussions over the perceived fairness of a progressive income tax may change from generation to generation, administration to administration, but the general principles being argued by each side remain the same. On one hand, you have the arguments that a progressive tax is fair because wealth is often a product of luck, exploitation of others, greed or corruption. Therefore, confiscation of large percentages of that ill-gotten gain is noble. Those who hold to this viewpoint will also say that a progressive tax system makes the fiscal playing field a little more level; no one has an audaciously large piece of the pie that they might use to purchase influence to safeguard or further increase their already exorbitant riches.

The other hand's argument purports a progressive income tax kills the incentive to work hard to produce and discourages saving and investing. Even if a person accepts that some form of progressive income tax is necessary, they may argue that rates that are too high are dangerous. Consider these words from Andrew Mellon, Treasury Secretary under Presidents Harding, Coolidge and Hoover: "When initiative is crippled by legislation or by a tax system which denies him (a taxpayer) the right to receive a reasonable share of his earnings, then he will no longer exert himself and the country will be deprived of the energy on which its continued greatness depends." Mellon believed that the income tax was a necessary evil to raise revenues to cover government expenses, but felt that it was repugnant to use the tax code to take money from an individual just because the majority think "he seems to have more money than he needs."

When Andrew Mellon took over as head of Treasury in 1921, the cost of living had increased over the preceding few years by 20 percent. Battlefield material - items such as food, fuel, clothing, and the like - had seen prices spike by nearly 50 percent. The "Great War" was over and with no enemy to fight, the public simply did not have the same level of tolerance for the idea of big government. Something had to give, and Mellon understood that. From 1921 through 1928, he helped orchestrate a bevy of tax cuts including repeal of the excess profits tax. The top tax rate was lowered through a series of tax cuts to well below its high of 77 percent. Exemptions for heads of households and children were increased, which eased the tax burden for many middle-class families. Americans received their tax relief, but the Great Depression of 1929 and the second world war that broke out in Europe shortly after, meant that tax relief would be short lived.

If this study of the history of taxation in the United States has revealed nothing else, hopefully, you now clearly see that national and world events greatly affect our tax policy. The first income tax was precipitated by a need for federal funds to pay for the Civil War. World War I hastened the passage of the 16th Amendment, making the income tax a permanent fixture in our nation. The scope and magnitude of that war brought about huge increases in the tax rates.

When the economic collapse of the Great Depression brought federal budget deficits, Herbert Hoover and Congress passed the largest peacetime tax increase in history - the Revenue Act of 1932. Franklin Roosevelt, when faced with the expense of waging World War II, reinstituted the excess profits tax and made the tax code more progressive by increasing the top tax rate and raising corporate tax rates (among other things).

Roosevelt told Congress in 1942, "In this time of grave national danger, when all excess income should go to win the war, no American citizen ought to have a net income, after he has paid his taxes, of more than $25,000." Can you imagine a sitting president saying such a thing today? But, time would show that Roosevelt wasn't just looking to tax the super wealthy; he was an equal opportunity taxer. By the end of World War II, the number of people paying income tax had grown from 3.9 million in 1939 to 42.6 million in 1945. Ninety percent of the workforce filed tax returns, and 60 percent of workers paid taxes. Collections rose from $2.2 billion to $35.1 billion.

But then World War II ended. History would lead you to believe that tax cuts were just around the corner, but cuts would not come for almost two decades. The Cold War and the expansion of domestic programs like Social Security meant that federal revenues needed to stay high. Presidents Truman and Eisenhower offered no relief from the high tax rates put in place during the war.

★　★　★　★　★　★　★

*"When there is an income tax,
the just man will pay more
and the unjust less on the same
amount of income."*

— PLATO (D. 348 BC)

GREEK PHILOSOPHER

★　★　★　★　★　★　★

★ ★ ★ ★ ★ ★ ★

"The nation should have a tax system that looks like someone designed it on purpose."

— WILLIAM SIMON (1927-2000)

FORMER TREASURY SECRETARY

★ ★ ★ ★ ★ ★ ★

★   ★   ★   ★   ★   ★   ★

"A tax loophole is something that benefits the other guy.

If it benefits you, it is tax reform."

— RUSSELL B. LONG (1918-2003)

UNITED STATES SENATOR

★   ★   ★   ★   ★   ★   ★

TAXERS, SPENDERS, AND REFORMERS IN CHIEF

President John Kennedy would be the first president since the 1920's to try to push tax cuts through Congress. He was criticized over the fact that his proposed tax reduction package did not include corresponding cuts in spending. Kennedy argued that federal revenues would not dip because "a rising tide lifts all boats" – he believed that lower tax rates would stimulate the economy and thus, increase federal revenue. His 1963 proposal would cut both personal income and corporate taxes significantly. Though Kennedy's assassination in 1963 meant he would not live to see the cuts become a reality, they were, indeed, passed in 1964.

Lyndon Johnson's presidency brought mounting governmental expenses due to the continuing conflict in Vietnam and the cost of the many programs that made up Johnson's Great Society social experiment. But, when Johnson went to Congress to try to get them to pass tax increases to cover these expenses, he found he was facing an uphill battle. The antiwar factions rejected any tax increases they thought would only go to fund another war, while conservatives rejected increases they thought would go to fund yet another big social program.

During the Johnson years, higher inflation led to a new phenomenon - bracket creep. Bracket creep occurs when high inflation brings with it higher levels of income. As incomes rise to keep pace with inflation, many taxpayers find themselves in higher tax brackets. Because there were no provisions in place at the time to adjust the tax brackets for inflation, bracket creep would prove to be a nagging problem for taxpayers.

Presidents Nixon and Ford's administrations did not push for any significant changes to the tax brackets. They chose instead to focus on tax and investment credits that would encourage saving and investing.

Then came Jimmy Carter. Jimmy Carter was a proponent of a highly progressive form of income tax. He despised the tax breaks he thought brought with them great inequity and made the income tax system, as he put it, "a disgrace to the human race." He wanted to broaden the tax base and crack down on shameful business deductions. Carter's Congress did not agree.

Senator William Roth of Delaware and Representative Jack Kemp of New York became the leading advocates for supply-side economics. Kemp explained the basics of supply-side economic theory: "By re-creating the incentive to work, save, invest and take economic risks by reducing the percentage of reward for that economic activity taken by the federal government in the form of taxes, we will have more investment and more economic risk taking. That will expand the total economic activity, expanding the tax base from which federal tax revenues are drawn, providing additional revenues with which to offset federal budget deficits." The significant majority of the population liked what they heard from Roth and Kemp. They felt burned by the government with the Vietnam War and Watergate. Meanwhile, inflation was eating up all their money driving up the cost of goods, even as bracket creep pushed ordinary households into ever higher tax brackets.

The election of 1980 was a political earthquake, as voters firmly rejected Carter's ideas and moved Ronald Reagan into the White House. Reagan endorsed the principles espoused by Roth and Kemp and advocated for across the board tax cuts for both individuals and corporations. He was quick to explain why he held to that position. During his time working as a motion picture star in Hollywood, Reagan agreed to appear in pictures each year until his income neared the point where he would cross into a higher tax bracket. At that point, he would refuse new scripts and take the rest of the year off to avoid the higher rates of taxation. He saw his example as proof positive that high taxes discourage productivity.

In 1981, Reagan signed the biggest tax cut in United States history. It was to be a three-year staged reduction with cuts of 5% the first year, then cuts of 10% in years two and three. Tax historian Elliot Brownlee points out that the Reagan tax cuts represented the first reduction of the income tax's role in the nation's revenue system since Andrew Mellon made his cuts before the Great Depression. Before the tax reductions, income taxes accounted for 63 percent of all federal taxes; after the cuts, they accounted for 57 percent.

The Reagan tax package did another important thing - it allowed for indexing of taxes. His tax strategy called for the current rate of inflation to be applied to the income brackets. This action all but eliminated the problem of bracket creep that had driven so many taxpayers into higher tax brackets. While this was great news for taxpayers, it was not such good news for the government. As long as there was no indexing for inflation, the government could enact "tax cuts" that were nothing more than adjustments for inflation. Now that automatic indexing for inflation was in place, if the government decided to lower tax rates, they actually would have to LOWER tax rates. No more smoke and mirrors to hide behind. In his book, *Contemporary U.S. Tax Policy*, C. Eugene Steuerle points out that, "By 1990, the inflation adjustment reduced receipts by an estimated $57 billion relative to the unindexed tax code."[4] Compounded over the years, the effect on

---

4   C. Eugene Steuerle, *Contemporary U.S. Tax Policy* (Washington, DC: Urban Institute Press, 2008), 82.

government revenues of this one simple change is astronomical.

While Reagan's tax package included some spending cuts, the cuts were not nearly deep enough to cover the loss of revenue from the tax reductions. Reagan may have hoped that the reduction in revenues would drive Congress to cut spending, but that would not be the case. Bracket creep had for many years provided easy money to the government. Now that easy money source was gone. Inflation continued to eat at government revenues even as programs like Social Security that were set up for what Steuerle called "expansion by formula"[5] grew unchecked. As spending continued, deficits soared.

It didn't take long for the administration to realize there might be some problems with their sweeping tax plan. The 1981 fall tax proposal was put forward to stem the growing loss of revenue. Rather than call it a tax increase, the Office of Management and Budget referred to it as "revisions in the tax code to curtail certain tax abuses and enhance tax revenues." The measure that finally passed was called TEFRA (Tax Equity and Fiscal Responsibility Act of 1982). TEFRA raised revenues by eliminating tax loopholes (unintended provisions that allow some taxpayers to avoid taxation). There were also significant measures in the act to strengthen the revenue service's ability to crack down on tax abuses and enforce compliance. DEFRA (Deficit Reduction

5   Ibid, 94.

Act of 1984) continued the work of increasing revenue by further improving tax compliance. By the end of the 1980's, the number of IRS agents employed to enforce the tax code was at an all-time high.

The tax code got thicker through each successive Congressional cycle. The cries to simplify the code grew louder and in the 1970s and 1980s, there was an increased push for tax reform. A proposal for a flat tax was given some attention in the Reagan era. The flat tax would be a consumption tax with only two rates - zero (for those with lower incomes) and a flat rate assessed to all other consumers. Fights over exclusions, deductions, and exemptions would be gone because those things would cease to exist. The administration thinly entertained a discussion regarding a flat income tax, in which a flat tax rate would be applied to all earned income. However, no meaningful proposals emerged as serious contenders. In the end, though there was much "discussion" of tax reform, no true reform was forthcoming - until 1986.

Tax historian Elliot Brownlee says the Tax Reform Act of 1986 was, "a process of restoring to federal taxation the sense of balance sought by the founders of the Republic," and "a major step in the elimination of tax-based privilege."[6] C. Eugene Steuerle calls it "one of the most sweeping tax code changes in U.S. history."[7] This reform brought tax relief to low-income households

6   Ibid, 124.
7   Ibid.

through increases in the personal exemption, increases in the standard deduction and expansion of the earned income tax credit. Work was encouraged. Previously, unemployment compensation was not taxable. With the passage of the reform act, those benefits would now be taxed, so the unemployed had new incentive to look for work - their previous tax break was gone. The 1986 Act eliminated many tax shelters (marginal or losing investments people made to avoid taxation) by the removal of various tax credits, deductions, and exclusions. The reduction in the marginal tax rate now encouraged investment in productive assets.

Any discussion of tax reform is going to include the mention of marginal tax rates and effective tax rates, so a clear understanding of the difference between these two terms is imperative. Your marginal tax rate is the bracket into which the last dollar earned in a given year falls. For instance, a single individual earning $50,000 per year currently has a marginal tax rate of 25 percent. You and I tend to think in terms of the highest marginal tax rate we pay as our "tax rate," but this is an incomplete and inaccurate assessment of our tax liabilities. Our effective tax rate is what we need to understand. Your effective tax rate is calculated by dividing your tax liability by your total taxable income.

For our single person earning $50,000 per year, the first $9,325 is taxed at a rate of 10%. The next earnings up to $37,950 is taxed at a rate of 15%. The last dollars earned to bring us to our annual income of $50,000 are taxed at 25%. Add that tax liability up and divide it by total annual income and you'll have the effective tax rate. Here's the math:

Taxable income	Tax Rate	Tax Liability
$0 - $9,325	10%	$932.50
$9,326 - $37,950	15%	$4,293.60
$37,951 - $50,000	25%	$3012.25
TOTAL LIABILITY $8,238.35		

Total tax liability $8,238.35 divided by annual income $50,000 = 17% effective tax rate.

If you'd like to figure your effective tax rate, you can go to your most recent form 1040. Divide line 63 (Taxable Income) by line 43 (Total Tax). If you file a 1040EZ, divide line 12 (Taxable Income) by line 6 (Total Tax).

With any tax reform proposal, there will ALWAYS be winners and losers because any adjustments to the brackets will affect different earners in different ways. What looks like a tax cut may not be a tax cut at all and what sounds like a tax increase may turn out to be a decrease for you. It all depends on how you generate your income and the way your income breaks down compared to the brackets.

Let's look at an example to help drive home the point. For the sake of simplicity, let's pretend the "Current Tax" plan in these charts represents where our tax law is today. Let's say Congress puts forward two tax proposals - Tax Proposal A and Tax Proposal B. Looking only at the highest marginal rates; you would conclude that both proposals are tax decreases, with Tax Proposal B offering the most substantial reduction. But when you compare these plans on an effective tax rate basis, you will realize that for an individual earning $100,000 per year, all three tax proposals generate the same effective tax rate of 29%. Are you starting to see why it is important to examine any tax proposal on an effective tax rate basis? Effective tax rates are unique to each taxpayer based on the makeup of their income and wealth.

Table 1

Earning $100,000 per year

Income Brackets	Current Tax (%, $)	Tax Plan A (%, $)	Tax Plan B (%, $)
$0-$20,000	5%, $1,000	0%, $0	29%, $5,800
$20,000-$50,000	10%, $3,000	30%, $9,000	29%, $8,700
$50,000-+	50%, $25,000	40%, $20,000	29%, $14,500
Total tax liability	$29,000	$29,000	$29,000
Marginal tax bracket	50%	40%	29%
Effective tax rate	29%	29%	29%

Let's advance our discussion one step further and take a look at how these tax reform proposals might impact another citizen. Assuming the same A and B tax proposals are put forth, what would happen to a lower income taxpayer, say someone earning only $25,000 per year? Here's the math:

Table 2

Earning $25,000 per year

Income Brackets	Current Tax (%, $)	Tax Plan A (%, $)	Tax Plan B (%, $)
$0-$20,000	5%, $1,000	0%, $0	29%, $5,800
$20,000-$50,000	10%, $500	30%, $1,500	29%, $1,450
$50,000-+	50%, $0	40%, $0	29%, $0
Total tax liability	$1,500	$1,500	$7,250
Marginal tax bracket	10%	30%	29%
Effective tax rate	6%	6%	29%

You can see that Plan A, though it would increase the taxpayer's marginal rate, would leave his effective rate at 6%. Plan B would subject this citizen to both higher marginal and effective tax rates.

Let's look at one more example to see how a higher income taxpayer – someone earning $500,000 per year - would be affected in our models. As you will see, both Tax Plan A and Tax Plan B illustrate sizable marginal and effective rate decreases for this citizen.

Table 3

Earning $500,000 per year

Income Brackets	Current Tax (%, $)	Tax Plan A (%, $)	Tax Plan B (%, $)
$0-$20,000	5%, $1,000	0%, $0	29%, $5,800
$20,000-$50,000	10%, $3,000	30%, $9,000	29%, $8,700
$50,000-+	50%, $225,000	40%, $180,000	29%, $130,500
Total tax liability	$229,000	$189,000	$145,000
Marginal tax bracket	50%	40%	29%
Effective tax rate	45.8%	38%	29%

I hope these illustrations help you realize that tax proposals are complicated and impact each taxpayer uniquely based on the structure of their income and wealth. Unfortunately, our representatives and special interests tend to over-generalize as they make their pitch for their pet tax reform plans. Don't let them fool you. It is never as clear or absolute as they make it out to be.

Let's get back to our discussion of the Tax Reform Act of 1986. The Act achieved some simplification. Since the standard deduction increased, fewer taxpayers needed to keep track of receipts to verify itemized deductions. Many industry-specific exemptions or deductions were eliminated, creating a more level playing field for all industries.

C. Eugene Steuerle, in his book *Contemporary U.S. Tax Policy*, explains that the success of a tax reform bill can be measured by how many hidden expenditures (tax breaks) in the tax code are eliminated or cut back. The Tax Reform Act of 1986 tightened 72 expenditures and repealed 14 expenditures. Steuerle points out that this number nearly equals all repealed expenditures since the advent of the modern income tax in 1913.

There was one more important change brought about by the Tax Reform Act of 1986 that we must mention and it concerns the taxation of capital gains. A capital gain is defined as an increase in the value of a capital item (a piece of real estate, stocks, mutual funds, etc.) above the price originally paid for the asset. These taxes are paid when the asset is sold. Before the Reagan tax changes went into effect, income tax rates were significantly higher than capital gains rates. Reagan's tax changes equated income and capital gains tax rates, LOWERING income tax rates to 28 percent while RAISING capital gains rates to 28 percent. This parity is an important and often overlooked portion of the Tax Reform Act of 1986. As more wealth moves into retirement with the baby boom generation, away from earned income, capital gains taxation parity could again be a focus for Congress.

Despite all the progress made by the Tax Reform Act of 1986, there were still problems to be resolved. The tax base, though broadened, was not yet broad enough to raise the needed revenue to attack the deficit. The continuing strong economy helped, but the deficit remained at $150 billion for fiscal year 1987. Then the stock market took a dive in October 1987. Immediately, deficit reduction became the number one issue on everyone's plate.

I've got to take a quick moment to point out how much attitudes have changed since the 1980's. Think back just a few years to when the stock market plunged in 2008. President Obama and Congress immediately proposed deficit spending in the form of a massive stimulus package. Certainly, President Obama was not the only president to engage in deficit spending to stimulate the economy - but his example is the one most people living recall today. Compare that course of action to the one taken after the market crash of 1987. No one proposed deficit stimulus spending, only the Omnibus Reconciliation Act of 1987. Though this act did little to affect the tax burden on individual taxpayers, businesses were affected. Loopholes were closed, and changes in the taxation of certain activities raised a bit more revenue to cut down the deficit.

The administration of George HW Bush (1988-1992) brought a slowdown in tax legislation, though the Omnibus Budget Reconciliation Act of 1990 included some measures to decrease the deficit. The Act included a "pay-as-you-go" (PAYGO) provision. The act sorted all federal spending into various "baskets" with spending caps assigned to each basket. For spending on a particular program to increase, spending on another item in that same basket would have to decrease. Spending cuts were realized through a decrease in defense spending (justified after the fall of communism) and increased controls on Medicare pay-outs.

More and more in the modern era, lawmakers and the office of the president have settled into a pattern. For each spending cut conservative Republicans call for that affects a social program, Democrats demand an equivalent increase in taxes on the wealthy or equal cuts in defense budgets. We see the same questions of fairness and equity in tax policy posed with the creation of the very first income tax are still relevant today.

Bill Clinton told the American people he was not your typical Democrat and his policies seemed, to some degree, to confirm that fact. His first year in office, he set about to enact measures to reduce the deficit. The Omnibus Budget Reconciliation Act of 1993 cut spending in much the same way the 1990 act by the same name had - by decreases in defense spending and increased spending controls, especially on Medicare spending. It also raised taxes on top earners, increasing the top rate from 31 percent to 36 percent and it increased corporate tax rates from 34 to 35 percent. The Act also included an increase in the gas tax.

The tax increases and spending cuts hurt and the midterm congressional elections of 1994 showed just how much. Republican gains helped them seize control of both houses of Congress for the first time since the 1950s. Emboldened by their gains in Congress,

Republicans proposed broad tax reforms, none of which gained any traction. Proponents of the flat tax emerged again, all advocating for a form of consumption tax, not a flat income tax.

One area that did see reductions was the IRS workforce. The staff added back in the 80s during the flurry of tax policy changes were now either reassigned or decreased through attrition.

Following his re-election in 1996, Bill Clinton set out to keep his campaign promise to lower taxes (spurred along, of course, by the new Republican Congress led by Newt Gingrich and his Contract with America). The work the administration had done to reign in expenditures during their first term enabled them to offer the first significant tax reductions since the Reagan cuts of 1981. The Taxpayer Relief Act of 1997 included a child tax credit. You will recall that a tax credit reduces the amount of taxes to be paid, which meant that this tax incentive only affected those who made enough from wages or self-employment to have a tax obligation. In other words, it was not a refundable tax credit. Refundable tax credits allow the filer to receive the credit even if they have no tax liability. The benefit phased out for those of higher income brackets, so it was still progressive in nature. The Taxpayer Relief Act included credits and savings incentives to help with the cost of higher education, as well as incentives like the Roth IRA and capital gains tax changes that encouraged people to save and invest for the future.

The IRS Restructuring and Reform Act of 1998 did attempt to deal with a myriad of problems at the Internal Revenue Service, though, in retrospect, not much was accomplished. Some work was done to improve the agency's technology to make them more efficient, but "some work" was not nearly enough. The IRS deals with some of the most complex issues in our nation, yet they are not given the resources to do it well. Add to that the fact that the tax code grows increasingly complex with each passing year, and it is no wonder so many taxpayers end up bringing their disputes before the court for a final decision on what the tax code "actually" says.

Historically, it seems like each addition to the tax law has generated two questions for every issue it tried to clarify. The book *Tax Stories*, edited by Paul L. Caron, gives readers a glimpse into the murky waters of tax litigation where these issues have been sorted out. For instance, we know we must pay income tax on earned income, but what constitutes "earned income" in the eyes of the law? Is income comprised of only those things the tax code declares to be income, or is everything income unless the tax code specifically says it is not? That question was taken up by the Supreme Court in 1955 in the case *Commissioner vs. Glenshaw Glass Co.* Ultimately; the Court decided that "economic gain is presumptively income" unless the gain is specifically excluded by statute. In other words, it is income unless the tax code specifically says it is not. What difference would that make, you may ask? More than you might think. In 1955, total income reported on the 58.3 million tax returns filed came to $1.81 trillion (in 2005 dollars). Tax liabilities on that amount were $219.2 billion (in 2005 dollars). By 2005, 134.4 million tax returns were filed on $7.53 trillion of taxable income, resulting in total tax liabilities of $980.3 billion.[8] The government brought in over four times as much revenue after the Glenshaw Glass decision as before.

Now that we're clear on what taxable income includes, another question remains: When does income become taxable income? *Eisner v. Macomber* dealt with this issue. For instance, if my employer gives me stock as part of my compensation package, is it considered income to me when received or when I sell the stock? If no dividends are paid while I own the stock, and I do not sell the stock in my lifetime, does that mean that part of my compensation package is never considered taxable income to me? What if I'm not an individual and instead, operate as a corporation? When are increases in my stock taxable?

What about if I owe money to a lender and my debt is discharged (meaning I am no longer responsible for repaying the debt)? Is discharge of that previously owed debt considered income to me? The Court would deal with that issue in the case of *United States v. Kirby Lumber Co.* (among other cases in this similar vein).

---

8   Paul L. Caron, "The Story of Murphy," in *Tax Stories*, ed. Paul L. Caron (New York: Thomson Reuters/Foundation Press, 2009), 56.

We may think that once we have clarity on the what and when of taxable income, that we are in the clear - but we would be wrong. We then turn to questions of what constitutes proper deductions when we are looking to lower our tax burden. What are appropriate deductible business expenses? (See *Welch v. Helvering* for a discussion of that one.) Which expenses can be deducted all at once and which must be capitalized over time? (*INDOPCO v. Commissioner* can guide you there - or maybe "guide" is a little too generous a description of that decision.)

Are you starting to feel like a dog chasing its tail? No matter how close we may think we are to "getting it," we never quite make it.

The Clinton administration focused heavily on deficit reduction during their eight years in power. Other than the failed attempt at the passage of HillaryCare in 1993 (healthcare reform), no big domestic policies were pushed. Many taxpayers found themselves entering higher tax brackets, not due to bracket creep as in the past, but due to real increases in earnings brought on by the strong U.S. economy. More taxpayers in higher brackets paying higher rates (thanks to the Clinton tax increases of 1993), meant the federal government was seeing an uptick in revenue. With no new large domestic policies to suck revenue from that stream, it is no wonder that the end of the 90s brought a projected federal surplus.

What to do with the projected federal budget surplus was a key issue in the presidential race of 2000. George W. Bush emerged the victor from that very contentious race, and he held that any surplus belonged to the people and returned to them as practicable. In 2001, Bush oversaw significant across the board tax cuts. It didn't take long for deficits to replace any projected surpluses.

First of all, pay attention to the wording I used - "projected surpluses." The government did not actually have an excess of cash on hand that was burning a hole in their pocket. The surpluses were projected, based on current trends. Unfortunately, current trends can and did change drastically. When on September 11, 2001, terrorist planes flew into the World Trade towers, the Pentagon, and a field in Pennsylvania, everything changed. The economy slowed significantly. Discretionary spending skyrocketed for obvious things like defense spending, homeland security, and rebuilding costs, and also for less obvious items like farm subsidies. In no time flat, those "projected surpluses" had been gobbled up by very real deficits.

The Bush cure for a lagging economy was more stimulus spending. The Job Creation and Worker Assistance Act of 2002 gave more tax relief to New York City to help them rebuild, renewed some tax credits that were set to expire and set in place some new deductions for clean-fuel vehicles. As the economy slowed again in 2003, the Bush administration doubled down with more tax cuts. Additionally, they passed a Medicare

Part D that established a benefit for prescription drugs. When speaking of the end of the first four years of the Bush administration, historian C. Eugene Steuerle says, "The turnaround from surplus to deficit was the greatest in U.S. history for so short a period (with the exception of the Civil and World Wars). Had the president's full time in office ended then, he would have been only the second president in the 20th century to preside over increases in defense spending and domestic spending, as well as decreases in revenues, all measured as a percentage of GDP. And the other was Herbert Hoover, who had to deal with the Depression."[9]

The growing budget deficit necessitated tough fiscal decisions. Steuerle makes the point that very few congressmen in office during Bush's second term had ever actually made tough fiscal decisions. "Many in Congress on both sides of the aisle had never enacted a bill that took away anything significant from anyone."[10] Lobbyists exerted their influence, often drafting legislation, shepherding its passage through the houses of government without consideration to whether it was fair or efficient. Give Bush credit for pulling together a panel to review the income tax system to see if anything could be done to simplify it and make it more efficient, but in the end, that panel - though they did draft two detailed proposals - was unable to get anything passed.

---

9   C. Eugene Steuerle, *Contemporary U.S. Tax Policy* (Washington, DC: Urban Institute Press, 2008), 220.
10   Ibid, 222.

Would switching the party controlling the White House from Republican to Democrat bring an increase in taxes? Not really. Barack Obama extended the Bush tax cuts during his administration. There were a few tax hikes on those in the highest tax brackets, but aside from some taxes meant to discourage certain behaviors - surtaxes on tobacco and tanning and penalties for not carrying health insurance following the passage of Obamacare - tax rates remained relatively stable.

Perhaps at this point, it would be helpful to explain why the Bush tax cuts required an extension during President Obama's time in office. Why wasn't the legislation permanent? Believe it or not, from the time of the founding until 1921, there was no legal requirement for anyone in our government to present a comprehensive budget within which the federal government would operate. Each agency operated on its budget with no central oversight. After incurring the massive expense of World War I, Congress was concerned about the efficiency of the federal financial system, so they passed the General Accounting Act of 1921 (also referred to as the Budget and Accounting Act). That act required the president, assisted by the Bureau of the Budget (now called the Office of Management and Budget), to submit a comprehensive budget proposal to Congress by February of each year. Congress would then appropriate the funds, using the president's budget as a loose guideline.

From time to time, the president would not agree with some of the appropriations made by Congress. When this happened, the president would "impound" or refuse to spend the money Congress allocated. Richard Nixon made such a habit of this that Congress passed the Congressional Budget and Impoundment Control Act of 1974. In that act, a provision called "reconciliation" was included to expedite congressional handling of tax and spending matters. To begin the process of reconciliation, Congress passes a joint budget resolution (an unenforceable framework for government spending that does not go to the president for his signature). If there are areas where the existing law does not fit within the spending or revenue limits of that budget resolution, reconciliation instructions are given to one or more congressional committees. Those instructions require the committee(s) to write new legislation that will bring the financial numbers into line with what is marked out in the budget resolution for outlay, revenues, or the public debt. This legislation is then voted on by both houses of Congress. Once passed, the reconciliation bill lands on the president's desk. Reconciliation bills are easier to pass through the Senate than other law because of specific guidelines spelled out in the 1974 act. Amendments to reconciliation bills are limited but perhaps most importantly, in the Senate, the debate on reconciliation bills is limited to 20 hours. No filibusters are allowed, which means a party does not have to have a supermajority to close debate and call for a vote. This explanation is admittedly a very simple description of the reconciliation procedure. It gives you a clear enough idea of the process so you can understand how the Bush tax cuts passed Congress at a time when Republicans did not have a supermajority in the Senate.

I think we've clearly established the fact that tax and spending bills are highly contentious. It's hard to get buy-in from enough legislators to get a measure passed. But, if a party controls the House, Senate, and the White House, thanks to budget reconciliation, it is possible to enact legislation strictly along party lines. That's what happened in 2001 and 2003 with the Bush tax cuts. Bush couldn't get buy-in from Democrats, so he and Republican legislators went around them.

But, lest you think that reconciliation is a sure-fire way to get around your political foes, you should know that there are some associated restrictions. For instance, unlike the Reagan tax cuts that were permanent law, the Bush tax cuts could only be enacted for a period of 10 years because of something called the Byrd Rule. Per the Byrd Rule, measures passed using reconciliation cannot significantly increase the federal deficit beyond a 10-year window. Since the Bush tax cuts did not come with corresponding spending cuts, they were projected to increase the deficit and, therefore, could not extend more than ten years. (Some of the cuts were in place for twelve years, but only because Congress voted - not in a reconciliation provision, but in a regular vote - to extend the cuts for another two years at the behest of President Obama.)

Since the passage of the Budget Act of 1974, 20 budget reconciliation bills have been enacted. As we've mentioned, two of the measures were the Bush tax cuts. Budget reconciliation was most recently used in 2010 to enable the passage of significant portions of the Affordable Care Act (Obamacare). Twenty-four budget reconciliation measures have been sent to the president for his signature since 1974; the president has only vetoed the bills four times (most recently in 2016 when congressional Republicans tried to use budget reconciliation to repeal many of the provisions of the Affordable Care Act). Though originally intended as a means for Congress to expedite their handling of tax and spending matters, budget reconciliation has increasingly been used to work around partisan gridlock.

A question I think we must ask is, are there drawbacks to passing fiscal legislation in this way? While the filibuster is a safeguard to ensure that all opinions - especially minority opinions - are heard before an issue is brought to a vote, is use of the filibuster now so out of control that lawmakers have no choice but to work around it? (It is worth noting that use of the filibuster has become almost a given since the turn of the century.) Is it no longer realistic for us to expect our elected officials to work together to pass laws that will give us well-thought-out, long-term budget stability?

But let us go back and finish our discussion of the Obama years. Interestingly enough, spending did not increase exponentially during the Obama administration. There were spending increases, of course, but President Obama's spending was somewhat restrained.

One figure did escalate tremendously during the Obama years - the federal debt. When Barack Obama took office in January 2009, the national debt stood at $10.626 trillion. On January 20, 2017, when he left office, the debt had ballooned to $19.947 trillion. As you look at those figures, you may be scratching your head wondering, if President Obama was not a big spender, why did the debt increase so dramatically in eight years?

To understand how we ended up where we are fiscally, it is necessary to know the difference between "deficit" and "debt" and how the two relate to one another. The federal deficit refers to the shortfall between what the government takes in through taxes, fees, and other revenue sources and what it pays out for programs like defense, Social Security, Medicare, infrastructure and the like. Each year, Congress is responsible for passing a budget. The problem is, Congress hasn't passed a balanced budget in a very long time. They set certain spending levels, project revenues, and right off the bat, the two numbers do not match. Spending exceeds revenue every single year. (The Appendices toward the back of this book contain charts that depict the situation for fiscal year 2016. Check them out.)

Our legislators and administration just determine to make up for the shortfall by borrowing (adding to the federal debt).

If you are a thinking individual (and I know you are because you are reading this book!), you know that kind of behavior is not sustainable - and yet our federal government has been living that way for a very long time now, and it is taking a toll. If you have ever lived on credit before, you know that the more you owe, the interest accumulates and your monthly payments are driven ever higher because of that. It's a vicious cycle. Now imagine that you are not dealing with thousands of dollars, but TRILLIONS of dollars.

Now those large monthly payments have you trapped; your ability to save for emergencies is all but eliminated. So what happens when a recession occurs, income levels shrink and tax receipts fall short of projections? More borrowing. What happens when an emergency arises, and the government needs to respond - something like a terrorist attack or a massive hurricane? There is no "rainy day fund" to tap. More borrowing. What happens when your debt-to-income ratio gets blown out of proportion? How easy is it to borrow when that occurs? Increasing debt levels bring a whole host of problems. It is clear we need to find a way out of this mess.

If you live with a household budget, you know that balancing that budget requires making tough decisions.

It means that sometimes you have to say "no" to things you'd like to buy - sometimes saying no to good, noble things - simply because there is not enough money in the account to make that purchase. If you have ever worked to eliminate debt, you know that in addition to reducing your spending, sometimes you have to take a second or even third job to bring in additional funds to pay down that debt. These are the decisions responsible grown-ups make. These are the decisions facing our nation today. Are there any responsible grown-ups left to make the tough calls?

Issues of tax reform are complicated; there are no simple fixes. Discussions of tax reform are uncomfortable. No one wants the blame for making someone else a loser in the tax reform game. More to the point, no one wants to make himself the loser. With debt in the trillions and no solid plans to balance the budget, some Americans probably feel the U.S. fiscal condition is hopeless. They are just hanging on until the whole thing crashes.

American author Richard Carlson said, "Many people believe that where taxes are concerned, they are victims, held hostage by an inevitable process that allows them no input, no control. This passive approach becomes something of a self-fulfilling prophecy; where people believe that they lack control, they seldom try to assert control." Let me be the first to tell you – you are not powerless. When the American people inform themselves and insist that their informed opinions be heard, change can occur. Just look at our history.

Take courage, my fellow American! You have managed to plow through 240+ years of tax history, and you've made it out alive. You are more informed that you were when you started this read; you won't be easily fooled by the partisan sound bites meant to lull you into compliance. People like you give me hope that there just might be enough responsible grown-ups left in this nation to right the ship.

APPENDICES

In some instances, nothing drives home a point like a visual aid. To that end, we have included a series of charts to help you see, at a glance, where federal tax revenues come from and where they go. The facts and figures come directly from the Congressional Budget Office and concern revenues and expenditures for fiscal year 2016.

In addition, we have provided a basic timeline of some of the history that has been covered in the book.

U.S. Tax History at a Glance

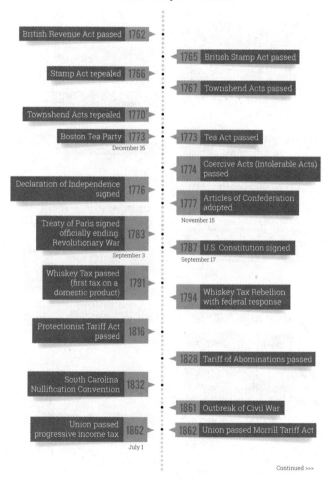

British Revenue Act passed **1762**

1765 British Stamp Act passed

Stamp Act repealed **1766**

1767 Townshend Acts passed

Townshend Acts repealed **1770**

Boston Tea Party **1773**
December 16

1773 Tea Act passed

1774 Coercive Acts (Intolerable Acts) passed

Declaration of Independence signed **1776**

1777 Articles of Confederation adopted
November 15

Treaty of Paris signed officially ending Revolutionary War **1783**
September 3

1787 U.S. Constitution signed
September 17

Whiskey Tax passed (first tax on a domestic product) **1791**

1794 Whiskey Tax Rebellion with federal response

Protectionist Tariff Act passed **1816**

1828 Tariff of Abominations passed

South Carolina Nullification Convention **1832**

1861 Outbreak of Civil War

Union passed progressive income tax **1862**
July 1

1862 Union passed Morrill Tariff Act

Continued >>>

U.S. Tax History at a Glance (continued)

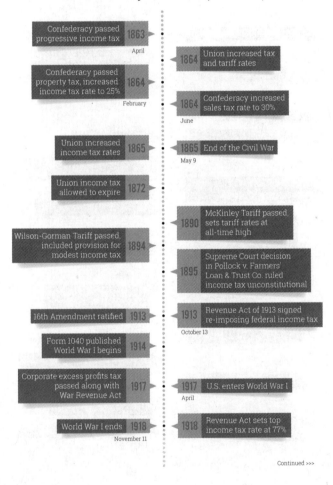

Confederacy passed progressive income tax — **1863** — April

1864 — Union increased tax and tariff rates

Confederacy passed property tax, increased income tax rate to 25% — **1864** — February

1864 — Confederacy increased sales tax rate to 30% — June

Union increased income tax rates — **1865**

1865 — End of the Civil War — May 9

Union income tax allowed to expire — **1872**

1890 — McKinley Tariff passed, sets tariff rates at all-time high

Wilson-Gorman Tariff passed, included provision for modest income tax — **1894**

1895 — Supreme Court decision in Pollock v. Farmers' Loan & Trust Co. ruled income tax unconstitutional

16th Amendment ratified — **1913**

1913 — Revenue Act of 1913 signed re-imposing federal income tax — October 13

Form 1040 published World War I begins — **1914**

Corporate excess profits tax passed along with War Revenue Act — **1917**

1917 — U.S. enters World War I — April

World War I ends — **1918** — November 11

1918 — Revenue Act sets top income tax rate at 77%

Continued >>>

U.S. Tax History at a Glance (continued)

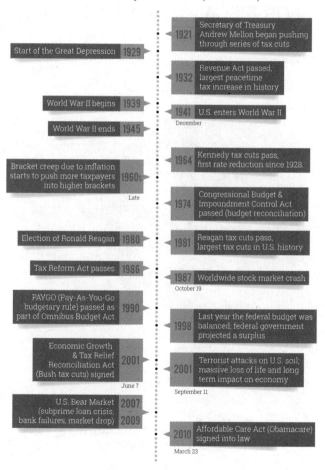

	1921	Secretary of Treasury Andrew Mellon began pushing through series of tax cuts
Start of the Great Depression — 1929		
	1932	Revenue Act passed, largest peacetime tax increase in history
World War II begins — 1939		
	1941	U.S. enters World War II December
World War II ends — 1945		
	1964	Kennedy tax cuts pass, first rate reduction since 1928.
Bracket creep due to inflation starts to push more taxpayers into higher brackets — 1960s Late		
	1974	Congressional Budget & Impoundment Control Act passed (budget reconciliation)
Election of Ronald Reagan — 1980		
	1981	Reagan tax cuts pass, largest tax cuts in U.S. history
Tax Reform Act passes — 1986		
	1987	Worldwide stock market crash October 19
PAYGO (Pay-As-You-Go budgetary rule) passed as part of Omnibus Budget Act — 1990		
	1998	Last year the federal budget was balanced; federal government projected a surplus
Economic Growth & Tax Relief Reconciliation Act (Bush tax cuts) signed — 2001 June 7		
	2001	Terrorist attacks on U.S. soil; massive loss of life and long term impact on economy September 11
U.S. Bear Market (subprime loan crisis, bank failures, market drop) — 2007 – 2009		
	2010	Affordable Care Act (Obamacare) signed into law March 23

WHERE DOES
THE MONEY COME FROM?

FOR FISCAL YEAR 2016 - $3.3 TRILLION

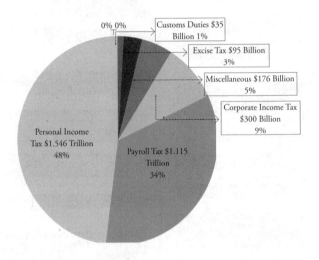

(Note: Numbers may not add up to totals because of rounding)

Source: Congressional Budget Office, February 2017

A HISTORY OF RECEIPTS BY SOURCE

(AS A PERCENTAGE OF GDP)

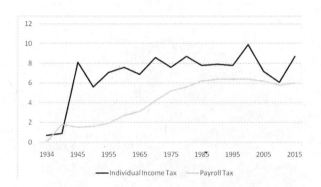

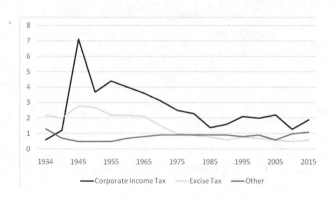

WHERE DOES THE MONEY GO?

FOR FISCAL YEAR 2016 - $3.9 TRILLION

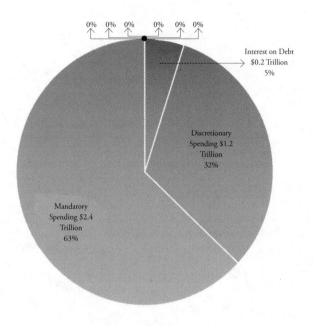

0%   0%   0%   0%   0%   0%

Interest on Debt
$0.2 Trillion
5%

Discretionary
Spending $1.2
Trillion
32%

Mandatory
Spending $2.4
Trillion
63%

Source: Congressional Budget Office, February 2017

DISCRETIONARY SPENDING

FOR FISCAL YEAR 2016 - $1.2 TRILLION

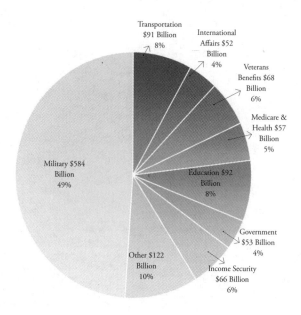

Transportation $91 Billion 8%

International Affairs $52 Billion 4%

Veterans Benefits $68 Billion 6%

Medicare & Health $57 Billion 5%

Military $584 Billion 49%

Education $92 Billion 8%

Government $53 Billion 4%

Other $122 Billion 10%

Income Security $66 Billion 6%

Source: Congressional Budget Office, February 2017

MANDATORY SPENDING

FOR FISCAL YEAR 2016 - $2.4 TRILLION

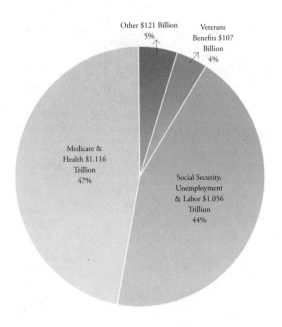

Other $121 Billion
5%

Veterans Benefits $107 Billion
4%

Medicare & Health $1.116 Trillion
47%

Social Security, Unemployment & Labor $1.056 Trillion
44%

Source: Congressional Budget Office, February 2017

DEFICITS AND DEBT

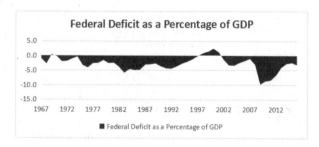

Remember, a deficit occurs when spending exceeds revenue.

In times of a budget deficit, the government must borrow from individuals,

businesses or other countries to make up for the shortfall.

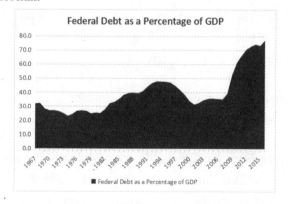

Source: Congressional Budget Office and Office of Management and Budget, January 2017

GLOSSARY

Capital Gain. An increase in the value of a capital item (a piece of real estate, stocks, mutual funds, etc.) above the price originally paid for the asset.

Capitation. A direct uniform tax imposed on each head or person.

Deduction. A reduction in the amount of a taxpayer's gross income that is subject to taxation. Examples include but are not limited to charitable contributions, mortgage interest, property tax, etc.

Deficit. A financial situation in which expenditures exceed revenue.

Direct Tax. A tax that is levied on the income, property or wealth of a person. A direct tax must be paid by the person on whom it is levied and cannot be passed along to another entity.

Discretionary Spending. Portions of the budget that are set each year by Congress in their annual appropriations process. Examples of discretionary spending items are defense, education, NASA, Federal Courts, national parks and many other budgetary items.

Doctrine of Nullification. Suggestion that states have the right to nullify or invalidate any federal law they deem unconstitutional. The Doctrine of Nullification has never been upheld in any federal court of law.

Effective Tax Rate. The average rate at which an individual or corporation is taxed. Calculated by dividing your tax liability by your total taxable income.

Estate Tax. A tax on your right to transfer property at time of death.

Excise Tax. Taxes paid when purchases of a specific good are made. Excise taxes are often included in the price of the product. The biggest component of the excise program is the tax on gasoline.

Filibuster. A parliamentary procedure in the U.S. Senate in which a senator may indefinitely debate an issue.

Gross Domestic Product (GDP). Total value of all goods produced and services rendered in a country over the course of a year.

Indirect Tax. A tax that is collected by an intermediary in the supply chain from the person who bears the ultimate burden of the tax (such as a consumer). Examples of indirect taxes include sales tax or value added tax.

Mandatory Spending. Portions of the budget that are required by pre-existing law. Funding levels are set and can only be changed by acts of Congress. Mandatory spending items include such things as Social Security, Medicare, and Medicaid.

Marginal Tax Rate. The highest tax rate from the published statutory brackets that applies to a given return.

Payroll Tax. Taxes paid on the wages and salaries of employees. One half of the payroll tax is paid by employees as withholding from their checks; the other half of the tax is paid by employers. Payroll taxes finance social insurance programs such as Social Security, Medicare, and Unemployment.

Tariff (also Usage Tax or Duty). A tax on an import or export.

Tax Credit. An amount of money a taxpayer can deduct from their overall tax liability. Examples include but are not limited to Earned Income Tax Credit, Child and Dependent Care Credit, Lifetime Learning Credit, etc.

SELECTED BIBLIOGRAPHY

This is not meant to be an exhaustive list of all the resources consulted as I prepared this work. This is simply a listing of the major resources I referenced. May it serve as a guide to anyone wishing to pursue further study on the subjects presented.

Caron, Paul L., ed. *Tax Stories, Second Edition.* New York: Thomson Reuters/Foundation Press, 2009.

Drake, Francis S. *Tea Leaves: Being a Collection of Letters and Documents Relating to the Shipment of Tea to the American Colonies in the Year 1773, by the East India Tea Company.* Boston: A.O. Crane, 1884.

Hoffer, Peter Charles, ed. *Dialogues in History: Benjamin Franklin Explains the Stamp Act Protests to Parliament, 1766.* New York: Oxford University Press, 2016.

Milazzo, Paul and Joseph J. Thorndike. "Tax History Museum," *Tax History,* http://www.taxhistory.org/www/website.nsf/Web/TaxHistoryMuseum?OpenDocument.

Stanley, Robert. *Dimensions of Law in the Service of Order: Origins of the Federal Income Tax 1861-1913.* New York: Oxford University Press, 1993.

Steuerle, C. Eugene. *Contemporary U.S. Tax Policy, Second Edition.* Washington, DC: The Urban Institute Press, 2008.

Weisman, Steven R. *The Great Tax Wars: Lincoln-Teddy Roosevelt-Wilson: How the Income Tax Transformed America.* New York: Simon & Schuster, 2002.

Zodrow, George R. and Peter Mieszkowski, eds. *United States Tax Reform in the 21st Century.* New York: Cambridge University Press, 2002.